Virginia, My State
Geographic Regions

Appalachian Plateau

By Doraine Bennett

STATE STANDARDS PUBLISHING®

Your State • Your Standards • Your Grade Level

Dear Educators, Librarians and Parents . . .

Thank you for choosing this *"Virginia, My State"* series! We have designed this series to support the Virginia Department of Education's Standards of Learning for elementary level state studies. Each book in the series has been written based on *documented facts at grade level* as measured by the ATOS Readability Formula for Books (Accelerated Reader), the Lexile Framework for Reading, and the Fountas & Pinnell Benchmark Assessment System for Guided Reading. Photographs and/or illustrations, captions and other design elements have been included to provide supportive visual messaging to enhance text comprehension. Glossary and Index sections introduce key new words and help young readers develop skills in locating and combining information. We wish you all success in using this *"Virginia, My State"* series to meet your student or child's learning needs!

Jill Ward, President

Publisher
State Standards Publishing, LLC
1788 Quail Hollow
Hamilton, GA 31811
USA
1.866.740.3056
www.statestandardspublishing.com

Library of Congress Control Number: 2011920558

ISBN-13: 978-1-935884-09-5   hardcover
ISBN-13: 978-1-935884-14-9   paperback

About our Maps

In Virginia, as in other states, there is no single definitive source of information for the designation of regional boundary lines. Such lines can and do vary based on geology, topography, or even culture. The boundary lines used in this book emulate physiographic or geologic boundaries as most commonly defined, *in toto*, by major Virginia universities and government divisions.

About the Author

Doraine Bennett has a degree in professional writing from Columbus State University in Columbus, Georgia, and has been writing and teaching writing for over twenty years. She is a published author of numerous books for children, as well as magazine articles for both children and adults. She is the editor of the National Infantry Association's *Infantry Bugler* magazine. Doraine enjoys reading and flower gardening. She lives in Georgia with her husband, Cliff.

1 2 3 4 5 – CG – 15 14 13 12 11

Table of Contents

Hi, I'm Bagster! Let's explore Virginia's geographic regions.

Appalachian
Plateau

Valley and Ridge

Blue Ridge Mountains

Piedmont

Coastal
Plain

The "Grand Canyon of the South" is in the Appalachian Plateau.

Grand Canyon of the South

Bagster is in Breaks, Virginia. He's visiting Breaks Interstate Park. He's standing on The Towers. The Russell Fork River is in the **gorge** far below. This area is sometimes called the "Grand Canyon of the South." It's located in the Appalachian Plateau, one of Virginia's **geographic regions**. The Appalachian Plateau is the western part of the Appalachian Mountains. It lies west of the Valley and Ridge.

Much of the Appalachian Plateau is in Pennsylvania, Ohio, and West Virginia. Much of it is in Kentucky, Tennessee, and Alabama. A small part of the plateau is in New York, Maryland, and Georgia. A small part of it is in Virginia, too. It is Virginia's smallest geographic region, but it's important to Virginia's **economy** and heritage.

A small part of the Appalachian Plateau is in Virginia.

Rugged Land

A **plateau** is an area of high, level land. The land in the Appalachian Plateau region is very high. It's about 2,000 feet or more above sea level. Some parts of the plateau are level and flat. But many streams and rivers have cut gorges in the plateau. **Erosion** from wind and water made the gorges wider and deeper. The many gorges and **canyons** make the plateau seem like rugged mountains.

Twisting roads wind around the steep gorges. Houses sit on small spots of flat ground. Vegetable gardens rise up stony hillsides. Forests cover much of the land. Part of this forest is the Jefferson National Forest. Laws protect the trees here.

There are amazing rock formations in Virginia. This is Stone Face Rock, near Pennington Gap. Can you see where it gets that name?

High, level land is called a plateau.

Plateau

Gorges and canyons make the plateau seem like rugged mountains.   7

The Russell Fork cut a large break into Pine Mountain.

Kentucky
West Virginia
Russell Fork
Breaks Gorge and Breaks Interstate Park
John Flannagan Dam and Reservoir

Breaks Gorge is the largest canyon east of the Mississippi River.

Rafting Through the Canyon

Breaks Gorge in Breaks Interstate Park is the largest canyon east of the Mississippi River. The Russell Fork of the Big Sandy River cut a large break, or mountain pass, into Pine Mountain. The canyon is over five miles long. It's at least 1,600 feet deep. Breaks Gorge stretches between Virginia and Kentucky. Daniel Boone was looking for a new way into Kentucky. In 1767, he found this single passage through Pine Mountain. He named the passage "The Breaks."

Water in the Russell Fork is controlled by the John Flannagan Dam and Reservoir. The **reservoir** is a large lake created for flood control. Engineers lower the level of the lake every fall. This makes room for water running off the mountains in winter and spring. Engineers release enough water to create white water rapids each weekend in October.

It's extreme white water in Breaks Gorge! These rapids are for experienced rafters and kayakers only. People have named some sections of the river "Twenty Stitches," "Broken Nose," and "Triple Drop." "El Horrendo" is a 75-foot stretch of violent rapids. It is one of the most dangerous rides in the eastern United States.

Valley on the Knob

The **headwaters** of the Powell River are in Wise County near Norton. The river passes mining towns like Appalachia and Big Stone Gap. It helped carve out Powell Valley. The valley is nestled in the High Knob Landform. High Knob Landform is a large and very old mountain mass. It lies in Virginia, Kentucky, and Tennessee.

The Cedars is also part of the landform. It's a very rocky and rugged place. It is a **karst** landscape. Water has eroded the **limestone** rock under the soil. There are sinkholes, caves, and sinking streams that go underground. Many rare plants and animals are found here, too.

Scientists at the Powell River Project have learned how to restore forests on mined land.

Visitors from around the world come to the Powell River Project near Norton. Scientists at the education center look for better ways to reclaim mined land. They use their research to teach mining companies new practices. They help students understand the wildlife habitat of the Appalachian Plateau.

Kentucky

West Virginia

Powell Valley

The Cedars

High Knob Landform

Tennessee

Powell Valley is nestled in the High Knob Landform.   **11**

Coal is burned to make electricity.
Coal creates jobs, too.

12   Almost half of the energy produced in America comes from coal.

Coal in the Appalachian Plateau

The coal mining industry is important to Virginia's economy. **Coal** is a **sedimentary rock** that is burned to produce heat and electricity. Most of the state's coal comes from the Appalachian Plateau. Each coal mining job creates three more jobs somewhere else in the economy. These are jobs like transporting the coal to markets, refining the coal, and providing goods to coal miners.

Almost half of the energy produced in Virginia and America comes from coal. Coal provides the energy needed to make steel, cement, and paper. It takes large amounts of energy to make these products. The chemicals in coal are useful, too. Methanol and ethylene are used to make plastic, fertilizer, and tar.

Coal is important to Virginia's economy.

A Fossil Fuel

Coal is a **fossil fuel**. It is formed over vast periods of time. A **fossil** is the mark or remains of a plant or animal that lived long ago. Trees and plants that once lived in swampy ground died and sank beneath the surface. Layers of dirt, rock, and water covered the dead material. Pressure and heat from those layers caused the decayed plants to become coal. We burn coal to make heat and electricity. That's why coal is called a fossil fuel.

Coal is a **nonrenewable energy** source. It cannot be made again in a short amount of time. Nature cannot replace fossil fuels as fast as people can use them. It is important to use these energy sources wisely. Scientists are also working to develop renewable energy sources, like wind energy and solar energy.

Coal is a fossil fuel. It cannot be made again in a short amount of time.

14

Coal is made from trees and plants that lived long ago.   15

Miners enter the mine through shafts and tunnels.

16   Coal near the surface is strip mined.

On the Surface or Under the Ground?

Coal exists in seams beneath the ground. Miners remove coal from the ground by **mining**. Sometimes coal seams are near the surface. Large machines uncover the coal and dig it out of the ground. This is called strip mining. It strips the earth away from the coal.

Some mining companies use mountaintop removal mining. Explosives blast off the top of the mountain. Bulldozers push the earth and rock out of the way. Sometimes they fill nearby valleys or stop up mountain streams. Environmentalists want to stop this type of mining.

Sometimes coal is too deep for surface mining. Then miners must use conventional mining. They must dig **shafts** into the ground. In conventional mining, miners drill holes into the rock. They enter the mine through the shafts and tunnels. They insert explosives to break up the coal seam. Continuous mining is faster and more effective. A machine with spinning cutters breaks into the coal. The machine's arms load the coal onto a conveyer belt. The belt carries the coal to the surface.

A conveyor belt carries coal to the surface.

To Market

Early settlers discovered coal in the Appalachian Plateau. But they faced a challenge—getting it from the mountains to the markets for people to buy. Railroads provided the answer. Loaded trains crossed the plateau and dropped into the Valley and Ridge. They chugged over the Blue Ridge Mountains. They climbed the rolling hills of the Piedmont and crossed the fall line. They delivered the coal to ports in the Coastal Plain. But locomotives lose power when pulling trains uphill. So railroads had to take longer routes through valleys. People built tunnels through the mountains.

Today railroad tracks crisscross the coal fields of the Appalachian Plateau. Trains take coal to power plants on the Ohio River. They take coal northeast to buyers in the steel industry. Other trains go to ports on the Chesapeake Bay. The Port of Virginia is the largest coal-shipping port in America. Large ships take the coal to markets up the east coast and overseas to foreign buyers.

Bee Rock Tunnel, near Appalachia, is only forty-seven feet long. It's one of the shortest railroad tunnels ever built. It is listed in *Ripley's Believe It or Not.*

Railroad workers had to tunnel through the mountains.

Trains take coal to the Chesapeake Bay for transport.
Large ships take the coal to markets.

19

20   Strip mining removes the mountaintops.
     An old strip mine can become a farm, a forest, or a lake.

Reclaiming Scarred Land and Dirty Air

People in America and other parts of the world need Virginia coal. It is a valuable natural resource. But coal mining can create problems, too. It can damage the land. Some types of strip mining strip away the vegetation and the soil. They remove the beautiful Appalachian mountaintops. This causes erosion and flooding. Plants and animals can no longer live in these places. Some coal burning power plants release dirty smoke into the air. Harmful chemicals in the smoke cause air pollution.

The environment is important, but coal is important, too. People all over the world depend on coal. Today people are working to find solutions. Researchers in the coal industry look for better ways to mine and refine coal and make it cleaner. Communities and environmentalists reclaim damaged land. Government officials work to find balance.

Reclaimed land in Buchanan County is now the Mountaintop Golf Course. It's on Compton Mountain near Pilgrims Knob. The golf course is covered with artificial greens. It's the first of its kind in the United States.

21

The Mining Tradition

Come with Bagster on a tour along the Virginia Coal Heritage Trail. It travels through seven counties. You'll see railroad trestles, abandoned mines, and reclaimed land. Ride by the **coke** plant near Vansant. Coke is used to make steel. It's made by baking coal at very high temperatures. Men shoveled coal into furnaces called coke ovens to make coke. The coke ovens at Vansant are just below the road.

Visit the Pocahontas Exhibition Mine and Museum in Pocahontas. Tour the mine with a coal miner. Get a close look at mining equipment and tools. See the murals in Clintwood and Grundy. Local people worked together to paint their heritage. Stop in Clinchco to see the Dickenson County Coal Miner's Memorial. The memorial pays tribute to the men and women who have died in coal mines. Visit Appalachia. It was a booming mining town in the 1800s. Today you can see the coal camps outside of town. You can imagine life as a coal miner, then and now.

The Pocahontas Exhibition Mine is a **National Historic Landmark**.

Men shoveled coal into ovens to make coke.

Buchanan
Dickenson
Wise
Russell
Tazewell
Lee
Scott
Virginia Coal Heritage Trail

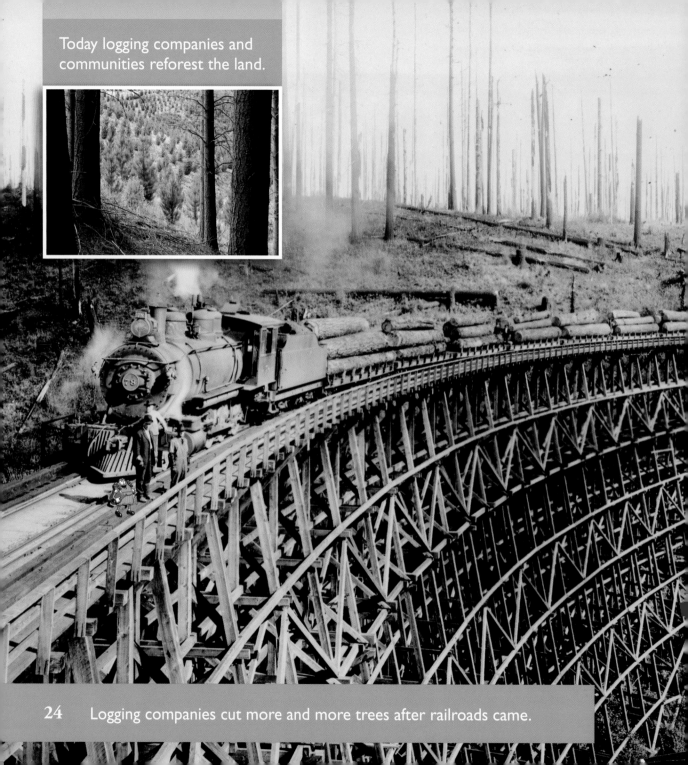

Today logging companies and communities reforest the land.

Logging companies cut more and more trees after railroads came.

Lessons from Logging

The logging industry played an important role in the economy of the Appalachian Plateau. Early forests were full of oak, beech, poplar, chestnut, and ash. Logging companies cut these and other trees. Horse-drawn wagons hauled the timber out of the mountains. After railroads came, logging companies could cut more and more trees. Sometimes logs were floated down rivers to saw mills. Mining companies hired loggers to cut complete forests from the land. Their families often lived in logging camps. The camps moved from place to place as the forests were cleared. It only took about fifty years before many of the big, old trees were gone.

Today forestry programs train loggers to protect the forests. Logging companies and communities plant new trees to reforest the land. This way there will always be trees on the Appalachian Plateau.

One walnut tree in Wise County measured over four feet in diameter. Loggers cut the trunk into four ten-foot lengths. It took six yoke of oxen to drag one of the logs uphill.

Appalachian Life

The Appalachian Plateau is part of a large cultural region called **Appalachia**. Today this area covers twelve states from New York to Mississippi. Parts of the Blue Ridge Mountains and the Valley and Ridge are in Appalachia, too.

Most settlers in Appalachia were Scots-Irish, English, or German. These early settlers lived off the land. Tall mountain cliffs and deep gorges often separated them from cities and towns. They learned to survive in the harsh life of the mountains. Appalachians took care of the family's needs. They grew their own food. They cut trees and built their own houses and furniture. They made dishes from pottery. They carved toys for their children and sewed quilts for their beds. They tooled guns for shooting meat. Appalachians are still known for their creativity, thriftiness, and commitment to hard work.

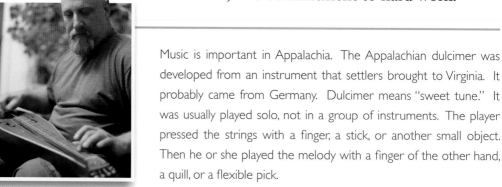

Music is important in Appalachia. The Appalachian dulcimer was developed from an instrument that settlers brought to Virginia. It probably came from Germany. Dulcimer means "sweet tune." It was usually played solo, not in a group of instruments. The player pressed the strings with a finger, a stick, or another small object. Then he or she played the melody with a finger of the other hand, a quill, or a flexible pick.

Appalachians are still known for their creativity, thriftiness, and commitment to hard work.

MY STATE

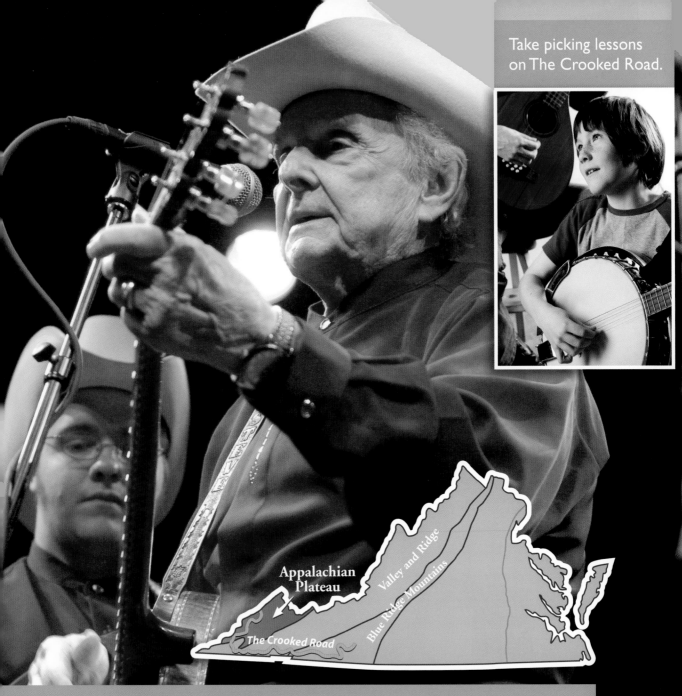

Take picking lessons on The Crooked Road.

Appalachian Plateau

Valley and Ridge

Blue Ridge Mountains

The Crooked Road

Dr. Ralph Stanley and the Clinch Mountain Boys made songs about coal country famous.

Preserving the Appalachian Heritage

Residents of the Appalachian Plateau keep their traditions and culture alive. The Crooked Road is Virginia's Heritage Music Trail. It starts in the Blue Ridge Mountains. Small towns across the mountains host music festivals. You can take picking lessons or clogging lessons at places along the road. Or you can just listen to bluegrass music. Dr. Ralph Stanley and his Clinch Mountain Boys host bluegrass festivals on Smith Ridge. They made songs about coal country famous.

You can visit the Ralph Stanley Museum and Traditional Mountain Music Center in Clintwood. See traditional mountain crafts at the Southwest Virginia Museum in Big Stone Gap. Nearby at the June Tolliver Playhouse, actors perform *The Trail of the Lonesome Pine* every summer. The play tells the story of life in a coal mining town. It is Virginia's official outdoor drama.

The Trail of the Lonesome Pine was originally a book. It was written by John Fox, Jr. from Big Stone Gap. The book was very popular. It was made into a movie three times. The play is the longest running outdoor drama in Virginia.

FRED MacMURRAY · SYLVIA SIDNEY
HENRY FONDA in
"THE TRAIL OF THE
LONESOME PINE"
COLOR BY TECHNICOLOR

with FRED STONE·NIGEL BRUCE·BEULAH BONDI·ROBERT BARRAT·SPANKY McFARLAND·FUZZY KNIGHT
Based on John Fox, Jr.'s Famous Novel · Directed by Henry Hathaway · A WALTER WANGER Production
A PARAMOUNT CHAMPION · Brought Back by Popular Demand

Glossary

Appalachia – A cultural region of the central and southern Appalachian Mountains.

canyon – A deep valley with steep sides, usually with a stream at the bottom.

coal – A sedimentary rock that is burned to produce heat and electricity.

coke – A substance produced when coal is baked at high temperatures. Coke is used in making steel.

economy – A system of making and spending money and supplying goods and services.

erosion – The process by which rock is broken down into sediment, or tiny pieces, by wind or water.

fossil – The mark or remains of a plant or animal that lived long ago.

fossil fuel – Fuel formed from the remains of ancient plants and animals.

geographic region – An area of land with similar landforms.

gorge – A narrow canyon with nearly vertical walls.

headwaters – The place where a stream or river begins.

karst – A region that has lots of caves or caverns.

limestone – A common sedimentary rock. It dissolves easily, leaving caves and caverns behind.

mining – The process of removing coal from the ground.

National Historic Landmark – A place of importance to the history of America.

nonrenewable energy – Energy from sources that cannot be replaced in a short amount of time.

plateau – An area of high, level land.

reservoir – A lake created for flood control.

shaft – A tunnel drilled into the ground to reach deep coal deposits.

sedimentary rock – Soft rock formed from sediments, or pieces of the earth's surface that have eroded.

Index

Editorial Credits

Designer: Michael Sellner, Corporate Graphics, North Mankato, Minnesota
Consultant/Marketing Design: Alison Hagler, Basset and Becker Advertising, Columbus, Georgia

Image Credits — *All photos © copyright contributor below unless otherwise specified.*

Cover – Tomas Bercic/iStockphoto. **4/5** – TheTowers: Minty Verbeten. **6/7** – River gorge: J654567/Wikipedia; Plateau: Photo courtesy Georgia Department of Economic Development; Stone Face Rock: Courtesy Rick Watson/Powell Valley News. **8/9** – Breaks Gorge: William A. Bake/CORBIS; Russell Fork: Reggie Tiller/Wikipedia; Rapids: Sebastien Windal/iStockphoto. **10/11** – Powell Valley: J654567/Wikipedia; Stream: US Geological Survey/Wikipedia; Scientist: Martin Jenkinson/Alamy. **12/13** – Coalfield: PamsPix/iStockphoto; Electricity: GM Vozd/iStockphoto; Miner: Darko Histrov/iStockphoto; Truck: Thaddeus Robertson/iStockphoto. **14/15** – Trees: Marek Kosmal/iStockphoto; Fossil: Falk Kienas/iStockphoto; Coal: Marek Kosmal/iStockphoto. **16/17** – Strip mine: Ad Shooter/iStockphoto; Miner & Conveyer: Les Stone/CORBIS. **18/19** – Railroad cars: Charles E. Rothkin/CORBIS; Workers: North Wind Picture Archives/Alamy; Ship: Teun van den Dries/iStockphoto; Tunnel: Ron Flanary, Big Stone Gap VA. **20/21** – Strip mine: The Mountaintop Removal Road Show; Reclaimed land: Harrison Shull, Aurora Photos/Alamy; Golf course: Courtesy Southwest Regional Recreation Authority, Spearhead Trails Initiative, St. Paul VA. **22/23** – Miners: Tomas Bercic/iStockphoto; Coke: North Wind Picture Archives/Alamy; Pocahontas: Brian M. Powell/Wikipedia. **24/25** – Railroad: Photography Collection, Miriam & Ira D. Wallach Division of Art, Prints & Photographs, New York Public Library, Astor, Lenox & Tilden Foundations; Replant: George Clerk/iStockphoto; Walnut tree: Print Collection, Miriam & Ira D. Wallach Division of Art, Prints & Photographs, New York Public Library, Astor, Lenox & Tilden Foundations; Seedling: David Claassen/iStockphoto. **26/27** – Quilters: Courtesy Georgia Department of Economic Development; Weaver: EFDSS/Heritage Images; Dulcimer: Tirc83/iStockphoto. **28/29** – Ralph Stanley: Rob Crawford/Wikipedia; Banjo: Dori O'Connell/iStockphoto; Lonesome Pine: A. F. Archive/Alamy.

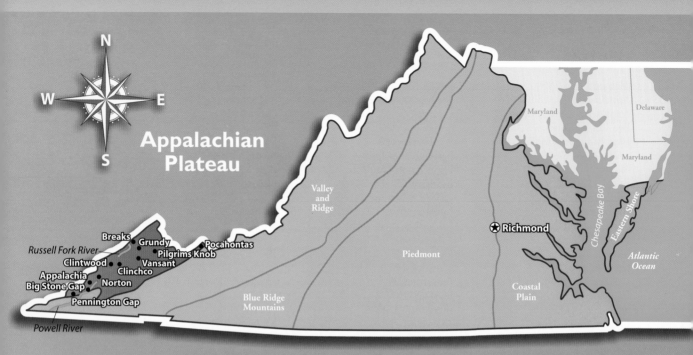

Appalachian
Plateau

Breaks
Russell Fork River
Clintwood
Appalachia
Big Stone Gap
Pennington Gap
Powell River
Grundy • Pilgrims Knob • Pocahontas
Vansant
Clinchco
Norton

Valley
and
Ridge

Maryland

Delaware

Maryland

Chesapeake Bay

Eastern Shore

★ Richmond

Piedmont

Atlantic
Ocean

Coastal
Plain

Blue Ridge
Mountains

Think With Bagster

Use the map and information from the book to answer the questions below

1. Coal is a nonrenewable energy source. It cannot be replaced in a short period of time. Can you think of some energy sources that are renewable?

2. Railroads take coal down into the Valley and Ridge, then across the Blue Ridge Mountains. Where might the trains cross the Blue Ridge Mountains?

3. If you were in the government, your job would be to make the best laws possible. Consider the issues between the coal industry and the environment. What law would you make to protect the environment? What law would you make to protect the coal industry?

4. Virginia's land rises as you travel from east to west. Where can you go in the Appalachian Plateau and be near the same level as someone in the Coastal Plain?